Geoffrey was born in East London in 1948 and grew up with his parents and two brothers in Winchmore Hill. He attended St Pauls C of E Primary School and, having failed his 11+, moved on to Winchmore Secondary Modern School. Here he studied for his O and A Level GCEs before taking up a place at City University to read Civil Engineering. A career with Consulting Engineers, Contractors but primarily Local Government served him well and, now retired, he lives with his wife in Buckinghamshire.

In memory of my dear friend, Ross, who had to leave us before I had the chance of sharing this book with him.

Geoffrey Ring

MUSINGS ON FAITH BY AN ORDINARY BLOKE

AUSTIN MACAULEY PUBLISHERS™

LONDON • CAMBRIDGE • NEW YORK • SHARJAH

A CIP catalogue record for this title is available from the British Library.

ISBN 9781035850655 (Paperback)
ISBN 9781035850662 (ePub e-book)

www.austinmacauley.com

First Published 2024
Austin Macauley Publishers Ltd®
1 Canada Square
Canary Wharf
London
E14 5AA

What's the Point?

I am a Christian who believes in God, does Christian things, and says my prayers regularly, so why do I need to go to church as well?

Is this the question that many have asked themselves but, as yet, have not received a plausible answer? Is this the reason why, in a thriving village of around 700 residents, that one Sunday, excluding the Churchwardens, vicar, and organist, I sat amidst a congregation of 5, yes, 5.

Perhaps the time has come to try and answer that leading question or, at least, just give some of my personal thoughts on which to ponder.

For me, I cast my mind back to the 1960s, 70s, 80s, and 90s. It was a time when my family was growing up and members were getting married, new additions arriving, and homes were being established further away, and it became more and more difficult to keep in touch. Yes, there were the usual cards at birthdays or Christmas or the occasional 'phone call, but it was something special that kept the family working as a family.

Enter my Mother! Matriarch of the family. A grand lady who had seen difficult times during the war when Dad was "away" but had always come out the other side, knowing how important families were. She was the one who, over the years, used to arrange family get-togethers, her open sandwiches were a sight to behold. She knew that by inviting everyone to the house and plying them with food and copious amounts of drink, we would talk, laugh, and make our own arrangements to meet up outside that gathering until her next one.

There were seldom any particular reasons for the "do's" but just the desire to see the family remaining as a true family. They were happy times.

Mother died in 1994, and we tried to keep the party tradition going. But it became more difficult as lives got busier; folk were committed to so many other activities with schools, clubs, work exhaustion, and business trips. At first, there were a few occasions based around special birthdays, marriages, or baptisms. But slowly, they petered out, and, of course, the Covid lockdown did not help!

It was only the other day when one of the family mentioned that they had not seen or heard from another for some time and wondered how they were. Yes, we still send cards at appropriate times, but the family is not as it was on Mother's day. We need to meet up as a family to stay as a family, look out for each other, and fully appreciate what family is.

This brings me back to the original question, why go to church? My view is that the Church is a family, the family of God. Unless we meet together, in person, to talk, catch up with one another, share stories, hear what has been written, and how others see God today, the family will drift apart. Soon those few who go now will themselves start to question whether there are other, more vibrant churches to attend where these interactions can bring them a greater understanding of "what it's all about". That would be a very sad day, and one, I hope, I never see.

Can we reflect on how best to get this message across? With God's help, I'm sure we can. Suggestions on a postcard, please ....

In the meantime, I hope that some of my ditties and personal reflections might help some to see their way through the ecclesiastical maze.

The reflections have come about following an invitation I received to join our parish Lay Team. This team organises and officiates at a Lay Led service on one Sunday each month.

The "ditties" I have penned have helped me to express my thoughts and feelings in a way I hope will allow others to think again about some of the aspects of the world of Faith.

Where Is He?

Envy is wrong, envy taboo,
But we need to be honest, need to be true.
I hear those extolling the time that was clear,
When God spoke to them, and they knew He was here,
Leading the way to where they knew they were led,
With a clear, almost audible, voice in their head.
But to me, despite listening for that voice that they heard,
There was nothing for me, not even a word.
In the quiet, still times when I thought He'd make contact,
Not a whisper came through......... was it me?

But then I thought of the times when things were not good,
And I struggled to know the way forward.
The times I prayed for that voice to offer the guidance I
sought,
But still, there was silence, is He really there I thought.
The ways to go forward just seemed so confused,
Until deep down I realised what I needed to do.
What was the right thing, honest and true,
What was the right thing to just get me through?

But perhaps those decisions that I thought that I'd made,
Which worked out so well, no longer afraid,
Were God's way of guiding me down the path He'd laid out,
His way of talking to me without having to shout.

Perhaps He works in ways which at times we don't see, or
hear,
But I now know He is there with guidance so clear.
And if we don't expect a voice as we know it,
Then let's not despair.
When you know what's right and the fog disappears,
You've heard Him all right, just not with your ears.

Reflection on Paul's Letter to the Philippians, Chapter 3:18

We hear of Paul's email to his mates in Philippi, and from the tone of it, I don't think it would have ended with a smiley face emoji! You can almost hear his disappointment when he says:

> "For, as I have TOLD you BEFORE and now TELL YOU AGAIN, even with tears, many live as enemies of the cross of Christ."

So it sounds to me as if he feels that they haven't learnt from what he's told them before. But in fairness to the good folk of Philippi, do WE ever LEARN from what we are TOLD? I'm sure if we search our memories from when we were at school, or if some of you are there now, where do we learn the most, especially about how we should act or behave, if we are only TOLD to do things… remember those days of:

Don't sniff, use a handkerchief.

Say please and thank you.

Sit up straight at the table… I can still hear my Mother saying that if I didn't sit up, I would have to wear an iron corset when I was older… happy days!

Or the classic – tidy your bedroom!

But how much notice did we really take, or did we just rebel, and I'm sure I can see a few classroom rebels as I look around. No, I believe we learn much more, even without being taught or told what to do, just by WATCHING others, even if at the time we don't realise it. Take note here, grown-ups with perceptive youngsters around them. I think Paul is saying: "look around at what's happening and judge for yourselves." In this way, he is encouraging them to focus on the good they see and realise, that perhaps, THAT is the way Jesus would have wanted it and, in so doing, they will start to be better Christians.

I still remember times in my childhood when I was learning without realising it at the time. My Father did a lot of his business with the Japanese and frequently we had a houseful of Japanese delegations being entertained. They were fun and really enjoyed the hospitality being offered. Mum and dad were great hosts, and there was a lot of laughter around. What I didn't realise until much later in life was what I was learning about compassion, friendship, and the understanding of others. Why do I say this... because my Father spent 3 years as a Japanese Prisoner of War.

So let us all try a little harder to do the right things, say the right things, behave in the right way, and be compassionate because that's the way those around us will, perhaps unwittingly, learn what Christianity really means.

It Really Doesn't Matter –
Just Come In

But where do I sit?
It doesn't matter.

How will I know what to do?
It's all in the service sheet.

What should I wear?
Whatever feels good for you, it's not a fashion show these
days!

Do I sit or kneel for prayers?
It doesn't matter what you do.

What if I need the toilet during the service?
There's one at the back of the church.

But I won't know anybody.
It doesn't matter.
You will be welcomed with open arms.

But I don't know whether I'm a Christian.
It really doesn't matter, just come along and see what you
feel.

I haven't been confirmed, what if it's a communion service?
It doesn't matter, either come to the altar for a blessing or just stay in your seat.
There are always those who do both.

I can't sing in tune.
Don't worry; there are others who can't!

I'm not free every Sunday.
It doesn't matter, just come when you can.

What if I bring my children and they make a noise?
It doesn't matter, we love to see children … and hear them!

I came once before and couldn't understand what the vicar was talking about.
Don't worry, many have times like that, it's no reflection on you.

But I haven't been invited to come along.

Well, you have now ……. See you soon.

Reflection on Romans 10:12 – 15 And Matthew 14: 13 – 33

It is most odd with you all wearing masks on not being able to make out your excitement, your engagement or your total boredom with what I will be saying this morning. I shall just have to use the advice I was once given that if the congregation start to look at their watches, it's probably time to wind up and if they start shaking their watches, before looking at them, then I should have already stopped.

In deciding what to reflect, on this morning's readings I made my first big mistake. As one so often does, I looked to the internet for inspiration. I googled (other search engines are available) the text and found myself deep in ideas, views, 1000 word essays all of which seemed to totally confuse rather than help. As panic set, in I thought, Why did I let myself get talked into this morning?" then, suddenly I realised the key I was missing.

One's faith, belief, and understanding are very personal things, and I didn't really want to know what all those teachers and academics felt. What was it that I got from the readings? Where is it that I get my Faith? And if I shared that, it hopefully might help others to reflect on theirs.

Reading from Romans seemed more difficult to me. It seemed to be telling me, which, interestingly enough, is particularly relevant at the moment, that with God there is no discrimination. As we heard read in the passage, the scripture says:

"… there is no distinction between Jew and Greek, the same Lord is Lord of all and is generous to all who call on Him."

But this raised a very good question by those listening:

"…how can they call on One in whom they have not believed?" and "How are they to believe in one they have never heard?" Or perhaps they should have added: "… one they have never seen…"

Perhaps a very good question for all of us. But sometimes we do take things on trust before we really understand. A child will know that if I drop this stone, it will fall to the ground; it trusts this will happen. Their birthday balloon full of helium will rise to the ceiling if they let go; they know it will before they really understand why.

A block of steel dropped in the sea will sink, but take thousands of tons of it and make it into a ship, and it floats.

So perhaps we can see something, believe in it, without fully understanding why initially. The real understanding and belief come later as we learn, become wiser, and, as it says in Romans:

"How beautiful are the feet of those who bring the good news."

Well, I'm not saying my feet are beautiful, and only you will decide if the news is good!

Matthew tells us of a time when things were pretty difficult for Jesus, to say the least. Last week we heard how

He received the news of the death of His mate John the Baptist, and He'd gone away by boat to a deserted place to be by Himself. We hear how He was followed by thousands and eventually, having spent time talking to them, and I guess answering loads of their questions, He'd arranged for the feeding of the 5000.

He must have been totally exhausted, and then He did a strange thing: He sent His disciples away, by boat, and stayed behind Himself to say cheerio to the crowds. Why send the disciples away and not go with them???

Perhaps He was just desperate to find a way of being on His own, as He then went up a mountain, by Himself, to pray. How often have we all needed time on our own, time to think, and perhaps time to pray?

By early morning, there were stormy seas, and the boat carrying the disciples was in trouble. So He walked out on the water, WHY? Why not just command the storm to cease? Perhaps He wanted to test His key followers, as, sometimes, He tests us.

Peter, who we always assume is "His rock," wants proof it is Jesus and not a ghost, so Jesus tells him to walk out towards Him. All is well until he gets frightened and begins to sink. Jesus helps him and says that well-known phrase (now I know where it comes from),

"Oh ye of little faith, why did you doubt."

He then gets into the boat, where His disciples also seemed to still have had doubts, but they finally say,

"Truly You are the Son of God."

If Peter was made an example of "little faith and doubt," perhaps there is hope for us all if we keep our eyes on Jesus and take less notice of threatening circumstances around us.

But our Faith can still be really tested, especially when we hear and see so many terrible things going on in the world. The news tends to be full of anger, tragedy, sorrow, and despair, and there is a tendency, even for the most faithful of us, to say in our darkest hours, WHERE IS GOD IN ALL THIS?

Perhaps all I can do is offer a prayer with which I will end, before you all start shaking your watches. It's called "Don't Blame God."

Don't Blame God!!

When we look at the world and see hunger and strife,
Hatred and violence and killings so rife,
When we hear in the news of anger and war,
With people not talking but shouting much more,
We wonder sometimes where God is in all this.
But wait,
Never let your faith start to dim, and certainly never begin to
blame Him.
Just remember:
He gave us brains so we could choose:
Whether to love or dislike,
Whether to hear or just listen,
Whether to comfort others or just ignore their plight,
Whether to grow food in plenty to share or just look on as
others go without,
Whether to develop science to help save lives or just plan
destruction,
Whether to put the environment first or let big business take
the lead,
Whether to think before we act or just rush in.
So, when things seem to be going wrong or bad things begin
to happen,
It's probably because the choices made with the brains that
He gave us are perhaps the reason, and not the fault of God.
He is always there; we just need to use and not abuse the
gifts He gave us.

Reflection on Luke 14
Verses 7 – 14

What is it Luke is telling about in the reading we have just heard?

Here's a clue:

(Let off Party Popper and Blower)

But more about that later. Firstly, I have a new word for you all to learn:

(Display Word)

ESCHATOLOGY (Pronounced ES-KAT-OL-O-GY) — altogether now — ES-KAT-OL-O-GY.

I'll come back to that later.

Right, Luke and parties, well actually a feast, but that's really only an excuse for a party. What he says is don't swan in and sit at the top of the table in case the host asks you to move further down the pecking order and you feel embarrassed. Instead, sit at the bottom and wait to be called to sit nearer the host.

This all reminds me of my time with large business organisations where each year there would be a grand dinner at fancy locations. The Guild Hall, Goldsmiths Hall, there were many others… all as grand as one another. I usually had to wear evening dress and looked like a penguin. But, there was always a table plan as you entered, and woe betide you if you did not sit where placed. I was usually, how do you say it, well below the salt, ready to await my invitation to move up closer to the Top Table… I am still waiting, by the way! It was very hierarchical. I guess that those invited were usually invited for a reason or in the knowledge there would be a return invitation. Me, I think I was just a member of the "rent-a-crowd" to swell the numbers.

But Luke is telling us that Jesus says… "no", don't invite those from whom you want payback or those who you know will invite you back. Your hospitality will then be repaid when they invite you back. Jesus does not say you shouldn't invite friends or family for a party, as I'm sure he would have done himself. What he is saying is, apart from those gatherings, at times, invite those who cannot pay you back, those who know that you know they can't invite you back so they won't feel guilty that they can't. He refers to the poor, crippled, lame, and blind. I think we can read into that just those who are less fortunate than we.

He is saying don't think of hierarchy and trying to better yourself, but think of those who need your help, who can't pay you back, for your reward will come in heaven.

Sadly, the Church does, at times, seem to be somewhat hierarchical and work against this… but that does not stop each of us doing our bit.

As my old friend Ignatius of Loyola said:

To give and not count the cost,

To fight and not heed the wounds,

To labour and not ask for any reward,

Except that of knowing that we do Your Will.

Now, really, I think that's all pretty clear… but, for the ecclesiastically minded scholars amongst us, you will probably have realised that this is all:

"The part of theology concerned with death, judgement, and the final destiny of the soul and of humankind"… Better known as: all together now…

ES-KAT-OL-O-GY.

Nobody Said It Would Be Easy

Nobody said it would be easy… faith, that is.
But you'd think you'd just follow the instructions,
but no, it's not quite as simple as that.
It's just like those flat-pack cupboards
where there's always bits left over.
The instructions you struggle with, don't understand, and
end up bemused and frustrated.

But I see now that religion's the same,
with the instructions not quite so straightforward.
Do I follow Leviticus, an eye for an eye, or Matthew and
love my enemies?
Do I favour my friends or the one who walks out, but then
returns?

Why didn't He make things clearer?

But perhaps we should just use the brains that He gave us
and relate things more to today.
We don't stone miscreants or sacrifice lambs;
We now work on Sundays and cut our hair.

So let's just act upon what seems right today.
Better still, read through all the instructions.
Don't leap in like you did with those flat-packs
and avoid that confusion, understand more.

Now, how did they start, the instructions, I mean?
With "In the beginning…" I think.
… Now read on.

Hi, My Name Is Matthew

Hi, my name is Matthew; I've been thinking a lot recently about my mate Jesus. You know, He's quite a guy. Not a lot of folk around here like me and, perhaps, I did used to add a little to what they owed in taxes to ensure I had just a few extra goodies in life… but then don't a lot do that? Anyway, He came up to me one day and said he wanted me to work with him and not only that, He agreed to come to dinner at my house. Well, you know, nobody like Him has ever been prepared to do that before. I usually just have my fellow tax collectors and, shall we say, dubious friends to eat with me. This was something quite different.

You know, it really made me think.

After he'd been, he faced loads of stick from everyone, but, I'll give Him His due, He held his ground. I remember he said something like sick people wanting doctors and not the healthy. He didn't really explain exactly what He meant but just sent them away to think about it and asked them to learn what it meant. Wow, He was good. No flaming arguments like I would have entered into, just so calm and clear as to what he wanted folk to do… and to be.

Well, it certainly made me think. And then he asked ME to join Him and help Him spread this idea, me, a disliked, and quite frankly hated, tax collector. But somehow, whilst I couldn't really believe it, something inside me said I should go with Him and learn more… So I did.

Gradually, as I followed Him around, I began to learn what it was all about. How He was the Son of God sent down to earth to save us all, to teach folk that to love is the answer rather than to hate. I learnt to value people's differences rather than despise them, to do good to others rather than harm them. As the years went on and I watched Him and listened to what He was saying, I soon realised what I had to do, how I had to change. It wasn't easy, but then He didn't say it would be. But I worked hard to be kinder, less argumentative, more understanding, I gave up tax collecting and cheating people and, eventually, I was even explaining these things to others myself.

But He seemed to make it so clear. He was clever like that. Now, how did He put it…?

Reading from Matthew 5:3 – 12

"Blessed are the poor in spirit,
for theirs is the kingdom of heaven.

4 Blessed are those who mourn,
for they will be comforted.

5 Blessed are the meek,
for they will inherit the earth.

6 Blessed are those who hunger and thirst for righteousness,
for they will be filled.

7 Blessed are the merciful,
for they will be shown mercy.

8 Blessed are the pure in heart,
for they will see God.

9 Blessed are the peacemakers,
for they will be called children of God.

10 Blessed are those who are persecuted because of righteousness, for theirs is the kingdom of heaven.

11 "Blessed are you when people insult you, persecute you and falsely say all kinds of evil against you because of me.

12 Rejoice and be glad, because great is your reward in heaven, for in the same way they persecuted the prophets who were before you.

Why Is It?

We often stand around in groups, perhaps a drink in hand,
To argue, discuss, promote or defend topics that matter to us.
It might be Brexit or Government plans, strikes or the NHS;
All have their ideas of putting things right and changing the
world for the better.

But in the end, still begging to differ, we respect their views,
remain good friends,
Top up the tankards, and move on.
There's no ill feelings or sense of pretentiousness,
Or wondering if the proponent has lost their mind,
Just a good debate amongst good friends who afterwards
remain the same.
But…

Mention God or religion or faith, and suddenly there is
silence.
Is this not something you keep to yourself,
Not something to promote or defend?

Why can we not express our faith,
Telling what it all means?
Of the times God's been there for us, when all seemed so
bad and despairing,
The times when we couldn't talk to others, but He was there
for the sharing.

Could we all not do more to share our belief?
Hold our heads up high and admit to our faith,
Tell others it's not a closed club for clergy,
But one with open doors for all.

Just maybe then the world would be a better place.
Let's try anyway...

Reflections on Mark 12: 41-44 The Widow's Offering

There are times when you're at a Church Service, and you get a reading that's incredibly long, and you don't understand a word of it. You have to wait for some erudite speaker to explain what it was all about.

Well, this morning, you have neither of those things. The reading you heard from Liz was short and fairly self-explanatory, and... well... you've got me.

Firstly, I have confessions to make on behalf of Richard and myself... The Church of England sets out various readings for every Sunday from which you can choose one. Well, last week we looked at the readings, disregarded them all, and chose our own. But as we haven't been struck down by a thunderbolt yet, and if nobody tells the Bishop, everything should be OK...

The key message from Jesus as he watched worshippers at the temple was it's not how much you give, but how much it means to you. There were those who, I guess these days, we would call millionaires, who appeared to give a lot, but really, while it was a large amount, it was probably only a fraction of what they had, or perhaps surplus cash.

But, Jesus doesn't condemn those who give more, as His teaching always said you should treat all people equally. He just points out that those who give large amounts don't necessarily deserve the most praise.

But perhaps there is a little more to the story if we read between the lines. Jesus doesn't even hint that what the widow gave was not really worth much in the grand scheme of things. By not saying that, perhaps He is saying that every gift, however small, is worthy of thanks.

To quote a well-known supermarket, "Every little helps," and it really does.

Many will know of the Parish Share. This is the amount we have to pay the Diocese each year as our contribution to the clergy salaries and various expenses. For this church, I think I am right in saying that it is somewhere in the region of £15,500 this year. A lot of money that has to be found from somewhere. But, looked at another way, if every resident of the village was prepared to contribute about 39 pence a week to the church, that amount would be covered. So we needn't be embarrassed about not giving too much because "Every little helps."

It is interesting that with all His teachings in the Bible, Jesus never shies away from talking about money. You will recall the stories of upturned tables of money changers, taxmen up trees, the parable of the talents, to name a few. But we, for some reason, do feel uncomfortable. It somehow feels awkward to ask for money; it doesn't seem very Christian. Odd, really.

But perhaps "it's the way you tell 'em" or more "how you ask 'em." I remember very well shortly after we had arrived in our village that I had a very friendly visit from the then church treasurer, just to see how we were settling in. We sat on my newly installed decking, drank coffee, and put the world to rights. All very convivial until he'd left, and I realised I'd signed his standing order form, but at the same time, made a good friend.

So, what's all this rambling about?

Perhaps Jesus is saying, give as much as you can, however small. Don't give with a flourish expecting praise from God; you can't buy a front-row seat in heaven, and "Every little helps."

Hi, My Name Is Mark

Hi, my name is Mark. I know I'm old now, but I was only a teenager when I came across this bloke called Jesus. At the time, I was still living with Mum and hanging out with my mates in Jerusalem. I suppose I was still trying to find my place in life when I heard Jesus preaching about what we should do, what we should be, how we should act. He was really quite persuasive. I found myself listening to Him more and more and seeing the hundreds of people gathered around Him, wanting to hear Him. It obviously wasn't only me that He struck a chord with.

I talked to my cousin Barnabas about Him and how He made me feel. Barny suggested that I join him and his mate Paul on their trip to Antioch. I suppose I was seen as their assistant on their mission to tell more people about Jesus. It started as fun, but then I decided that I didn't want to go on working with them when they went to Pamphylia. Barnabas had tried to persuade me to stay, but Paul wouldn't hear of it, thought I'd betrayed them, so I went back to Jerusalem where it had all started.

I know I wasn't one of the famous 12 Apostles, but that really didn't matter. There were about 70 of us chosen by Jesus to go out and spread the word, and that was good enough for me.

My mother stayed in touch with Jesus until the end, even offering her upstairs room to hold His last supper. Not that we knew then that it was to be His last. I remember well the chaos in the Garden of Gethsemane when the soldiers came. They nearly got me as well, but I managed to wriggle free and ran off stark naked — what a sight that was.

That was certainly a new beginning for me. I went off to Alexandria and founded the Church in Egypt, where I even became their first Bishop, quite a change from that teenager all those years ago. You just never know where knowing Jesus leads you... I certainly didn't.

The Buzz That Is Church

I went to church the other day but couldn't find a seat,
The church was full and buzzed with life,
Excited children running rife.
Mums and Dads sharing tales of the week,
Books handed out, vicar ready to speak.

As the service progressed, the hymns rang out,
Joyous voices of all giving praise for the life
Of the One up above, looking down on His people,
Enjoying themselves in praise of His name.

The vicar related the readings to life,
All understood the relevance today.
The prayers offered up gave thanks for the blessings
That many enjoyed,
But thoughts also shared for those not as lucky,
Whose lives were in need of our care.

And after the service, at coffee, we chatted,
We laughed and exchanged our stories.

But then, amidst the throng, I felt hands on my shoulders,
I tried to ignore them, but their shaking persisted,
Then a voice seemed to echo in my ears,

"Wake up, wake up, we're going to be late,
It's 9:00 already; we need to be off."
I dressed double quick and raced to the church,
Would I find a seat?

As we joined the few there, I thought of my dream,
Could it one day be a reality?
We can only pray that it might,
But now, yes, there was a seat..........

Luke

Hi, my name is Luke. Many people think I was one of Jesus' first disciples, but, actually, I never knew Him personally. I only began to realise what He was all about when I started travelling around with Paul.

I was just a doctor, born in Antioch, when I met Paul. He was looking for someone to go with him on his travels, someone who could read and write and was good with words... and I seemed to fit the bill. He was very persuasive! Our first trip together was to Greece; I met him in Troas, must have been around AD51; I was about 40 by then. We travelled around to Macedonia and onto Philippi. I was tasked with keeping diaries of our trips so others could know all about Jesus and what He stood for.

While I was not one to know Jesus personally, I was lucky enough to have known His mother, Mary. She told me a lot about the birth of Jesus and lots of the stories of His early life, which I felt I should write about. Perhaps that was why I also felt I needed to write so much about all the other women who used to accompany Jesus on His travels. There were many of them like Mary Magdalene, Joanna, Susanna, and Martha, and they all, along with many others, were happy to use their own resources to help Jesus and His disciples.

Apart from helping to spread the word working with Paul, I did find enough time to paint, something I really enjoyed. I specialised in icons and even managed one of Mary and her child. Let's hope it's still around in years to come for others to enjoy.

I must admit that I am feeling very tired now, but then, at nearly 84, I suppose I haven't done badly. I knew that, after my last trip with Paul on his final expedition to Jerusalem, it would be difficult to carry on like that forever.

I have witnessed so many things over the years, and I have never regretted giving up the medical profession. From those early days of knowing very little about the wonder of Jesus' teaching and learning of how strong Faith can sustain you, especially when the going gets tough, I just hope that those who follow afterwards will be able to rejoice in all that as well.

Reflections on Luke 11: 1 – 4
Jesus, Teach Us How to Pray

Some things I never really understand! Whilst it was a very short reading from Luke this morning, it is one that has always puzzled me. The disciples, having been with Jesus for ages, followed Him around, heard Him preach, heard Him pray, say to Him… "…Teach US how to pray…"

Wouldn't you have thought that they might have twigged how to do that? But no, they felt obliged to ask.

Having rashly said I would try and reflect on that reading, it meant that I had to really think about things.

What first came to mind was that it must have taken some courage to admit to the boss that they really didn't understand what they had to do to pray. Perhaps there is a message there for all of us, that sometimes we need to be really honest with ourselves and admit that we don't understand what everyone else seems to, or we can't follow what everyone else seems to be nodding their heads in agreement with. But if there is nothing else I have learnt over the years, I have realised that sometimes, for those old enough to remember Danny Kaye and his song about "The King's New Clothes", you may not be the only one.

This I twigged many years ago when sitting in on a very erudite lecture at the Institute of Civil Engineers. By the break, I had understood nothing and had no idea what the speaker was on about. I plucked up the courage to say to the chap next to me, "You know, I have no idea what he was on about," to which he replied, "I'm glad you said that because neither did I". So, always be honest and admit when there are things you don't understand... just like the disciples did.

Of course, in teaching them how to pray and what to say, the reading just gives you the words, not how to say them. How many times have we said the Lord's Prayer, 1000's I would suggest, how often now is it a case of:

(AS FAST AS POSS WITH NO MEANING) Our Father... Amen. I used to stand next to our Group Scout Leader at parade when I was about 14/15, and I remember to this day what he said:

OUR Father who art **IN** heaven
HALLOWED be **THY** name
THY kingdom come
THY WILL be done
On **EARTH** as it is in **HEAVEN**
Give us **THIS** day **OUR** daily bread
Forgive us **OUR** trespasses as **WE** forgive **THOSE** who trespass against **US**
Lead us **NOT** into **TEMPTATION** but
Deliver **US** from **EVIL**
For **THINE IS** the kingdom
The **POWER AND** the **GLORY**
For **EVER** and **EVER**
Amen.

My Name Is John

Hi, my name is John. I was only 24 and still living at home with my folks in Bethsaida when I met Jesus. I used to work with my brother James in partnership with Andrew and Peter in their fishing business. I suppose I became sort of a personal agent for Jesus and used to look after His family affairs, which I continued to do until His mother, Mary, died.

Jesus really seemed to father me, which I guess was because I was the youngest of all His disciples and, after all, my brothers and I had known Jesus for longer than any of the others.

When Andrew was made a sort of director of Jesus' group, he was asked to assign two or three of us to be with Him and to remain by His side, to comfort Him and to minister to His daily needs. In the end, Andrew chose me along with Peter and James to do that. I was so proud.

As I grew older, whilst I tried to be good, many said that I was somewhat conceited, but then we can't all be perfect, can we? But what I know I always was, was dependable, faithful, and devoted to Jesus, and I think He realised that.

What always humbled me was the way Jesus was happy to go around without a home himself, having made provision for the care of His mother and family. What I think also changed me in those years with the Boss was His undying faith in the Father in Heaven and His daily life of implicit trust. It was really something to behold and something I tried so hard to emulate.

I know that I was sometimes intolerant and had to resist the urge of calling down fire from heaven on the heads of those disrespectful Samaritans. But I did learn that that was not perhaps the best way forward.

I clearly remember those last days with Jesus. I was the one who followed Him to His final arrest, was there as He suffered on the cross, and listened carefully to what instructions He might have for me at the end.

I never suffered as much as He did, of course, all I had to put up with was a few prison sentences and a temporary exile to Patmos. Although, whilst there, I did take the time to write the Book of Revelation, and I hope it will remain with the scholars for years to come.

After much travelling, I decided to settle in Ephesus when I was appointed as Bishop of the Asia churches. I had an associate then who I tasked with the job of putting my recollections into words, my Gospel I suppose, with tales of a long and rewarding life. I'm 99 years old now, but I hope I've got another couple of years in me yet. We shall see…

Reflection on John 20
Verses 19 – 31

Sometimes I feel a bit of a fraud! Scholars over the years have spent their lives studying certain Bible passages, researching for their PhDs, and writing books on key events in Jesus' life. And here I am, just a bloke who rashly agreed to join the Lay Team a few years ago, standing here and trying to sound as if he knows what he's talking about.

However, what I do know, and can say with confidence, is that what I say is what I really believe, whether or not it bears any relationship to what Jesus was about or whether it resonates with your thinking. But more importantly, it's what helps ME with my faith.

In our reading, we heard about Thomas and his initial total disbelief that his mates had actually seen Jesus. Thomas does seem to get a bit of a bad press, but you can't really blame him for his initial doubts. Had any of the other 12 not been at that first visit of the Risen Christ, would they not have reacted in a similar way? But Jesus seemed to feel He had to prove a point and appeared a second time when Thomas was there. But, actually, it wasn't just Thomas who was being made a bit of a scapegoat, for in Corinthians Chapter 15, Paul reports that:

"… Then Jesus appeared to more than 500 brothers and sisters at one time… Then He appeared to James, then to all the apostles. Last of all… He appeared to me."

Now, not a lot of people know that!

So, I suppose these days it would be something like a final tour. But throughout, I am sure He kept making the point, as He did in His first appearance to the 12, that:

"... Have you believed it because you have SEEN Me? Blessed are those who have not seen and yet have come to believe."

It seems to be the key message that John wants to stress in his gospel is about blind faith, faith without necessarily seeing or not yet fully understanding. Faith in God that Jesus taught about. Faith that we all can find in many strange ways, and sometimes, at the most odd times. Faith that will keep us going through this complicated world we now live in and Faith that will lead us to join those who have gone before when we also leave the world we know.

Or to finish with another extract from John:

"For God so loved the world, that He gave His only Son, that whoever believes in Him should not perish but have eternal life."

Amen.

Surely It Must Be True ...

He had no Tweets or TikTok, he didn't have a Blog,
No online sites for "likes" to tick or apps to spread the word,
No influencing websites or streams of daily news,
Just 12 good men to work with Him and learn about His
views.

Yet, somehow, unlike the Beatles, Elvis, and Rolling Stones,
Who had such fame and fortune and were always so well-
known,
Who we thought would reign forever and never be forgotten,
But whose names mean little now to so many folk around,
Jesus' name is one that's lived on for two thousand years,
Is still remembered, talked about, and known both far and
wide.

We still discuss His stories, His life, and what He'd say,
He is still there in the minds of many despite His simple
start.
So surely there is something in this talk of Faith,
The strength and power it gives.

Surely He is "up there", looks down on us, and lives.

Reflection on Matthew
Chapter 11, Verses 16 – 19
And 25 – 30

Sometimes I wonder, "Is it me?" Why did Jesus never seem to say what he meant in ways I could understand? Parables, parables, always parables. Now, you might think that by doing it like that, it would help those listening to better understand what His message was.

So I say again, "Is it me?"

The one thing I suppose it does do, in not being too obvious at first sight, is that it makes you really look at, and study, what the true message was. Which, I have to confess, is what I had to do last week before I began to see the light from the trees, and even then, it was only a very dim light.

It seems that Jesus, when referring to children… "Sitting in the MarketPlace"… is saying that sometimes children cannot decide what to play, whether Weddings or Funerals. Or, as He puts it:

"We played the pipe for you, and you did not dance.
We sang a dirge, and you did not mourn."
And in the end, they ended up playing neither.

He seems to use this analogy to help us see that when John came, he was seen as a bit austere and therefore no one listened to him, and when Jesus came and was eating, drinking, and partying with sinners, they didn't like that either and ended up, just like the children who couldn't make their minds up what to play, following neither.

But the reading goes on to say:

"Wisdom is proved right by her deeds."

And Jesus' own deeds give evidence that He reveals the wisdom of God, that He is the One who WAS meant to come and the One who does usher in God's Kingdom.

So IS He saying watch, listen, learn but don't prejudge? You will then realise what to do... or play. No doubt some ecclesiastical guru would answer that question for you, I'm just the guy who asks it!

The reading then ends with more confusion:

"... and no one knows the Father except the Son and those to whom the Son chooses to reveal Him."

It sounds as if Jesus has chosen to reveal things to "infants" and not to the wise and intelligent. The infants He refers to are probably the poor, meek, and mild who, somewhere else I seem to recall, He called Blessed and hid them from the wise and intelligent, referring to the religious leaders, scribes, and Pharisees.

And it seems that Jesus Himself admits that it isn't going to be easy as the reading finishes by saying:

"Come to me, all you who are weary and burdened, and I will give you rest. Take my yoke upon you and learn from me, for I am gentle and humble at heart, and you will find rest for your souls. For my yoke is easy and my burden is light."

Here I think He is saying lay your burden, or yokes, on Me and I will support you.

In conclusion... or confusion, what have we learnt:

This Faith lark isn't easy.

Nothing is quite straightforward.

Follow the ones you see doing the right thing and do the same.

Don't prejudge, even unconsciously, albeit sometimes that's very difficult and something we do without even realising it....

Which I say with a certain degree of guilt, for it reminds me of a programme I was listening to on the radio when driving somewhere. The Interviewer was speaking to a fellow who, from the sound of his voice, I guessed was sort of African and probably black. I listened on without thinking about anything in particular, and I can't even remember what the interview was about. As the discussion progressed, the interviewer mentioned that this guy was a professor in something at a top university. My immediate reaction was, "Wow, that's a surprise." Immediately, I felt ashamed at my reaction. Somehow, subconsciously, I pictured him in my mind as someone who couldn't possibly have such a role. So, I'm afraid, M' Lord, Guilty as charged....

And finally:

In times of stress, anguish, or despair, look to lay your yoke, or troubles, in Christ.

AMEN.

The Journey

"It's time to go."
"I don't want to go."
"You will do as you're told."
"But I'd rather stay at home and play."
"You can play when you get home."
"It's not fair, you don't have to go."
"Just get changed, do as you're told, you are going."

This was the gist of conversations I had as a 5-year-old at quarter to three on a Sunday afternoon every week as I was about to be sent to Sunday school. I hated it and could not understand why I was being sent to school on a Sunday when my parents were enjoying themselves at home. In those days, you didn't debate the ethics of this unreasonable approach of your parents. Then, in the end, you just did as you were told.

I suppose my main dislike of the idea was the emphasis on the word "School", which it certainly was. We had an attendance register, annual prize-giving if you attended regularly,

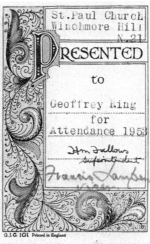

and exams on what you had learnt each term. I recall once even losing marks in my exam for doodling in the margins! Also, thinking back, it probably didn't help that I didn't relate what I was doing to Church as my parents never went there. I suppose I was just sent to Sunday school because "that's what you did" as parents then.

What I didn't appreciate at the time was that this was the start of a journey I was embarking upon. A journey that was to be long, one where the end never seemed to be in sight, and one which I feel I am still on to this day.

Having survived my time at Sunday school, and given up rebelling when I realised there was little chance of getting my own way, the time came for my Confirmation lessons, more instruction. By now I was 12 years old and beginning to see the point of the journey but still not really realising I was on it. Having been confirmed, I was approached by the vicar and "asked" if I would like to be a server in church. It sounded important, so I agreed, one thing led to another, and before long, the Church started to have quite a meaning for me.

The years rolled on, age beckoned, marriage came, children came, and careers developed. During this time, church-going tended to be somewhat intermittent and was worked around family commitments.

As we became fairly settled with two small children, the Sunday school entered my life again. "Would I just help occasionally", the vicar asked? This was a slippery slope I found as I ended up as Sunday School Superintendent.

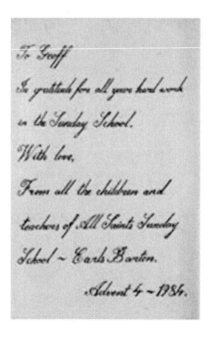

To Geoff

In gratitude for all your hard work in the Sunday School.

With love,

From all the children and teachers of All Saints Sunday School ~ Earls Barton.

Advent 4 ~ 1984.

Looking back now, I can see that the journey I had been dispatched upon all those years ago was well underway and the destination, whilst not very clear, was perhaps something to seek out. Interestingly enough, and this is an important message to Clergy, had it been suggested at that stage that I consider ordination, my life, and journey, may well have taken a completely different route. As it was, the suggestion was never made, and so that remains a "what if"?

My journey still had miles to run, but, as it did, I came to realise how important it was and how grateful I was to the parents of that truculent 5-year-old all those years ago. My faith in God gradually became stronger, and the foundations I'd received from those early Sunday school teachers, who I so disliked, proved priceless for me. As the years went on, life seemed to get more difficult, and at times really tested my faith to the limit. There were plenty of good times, but sometimes the black clouds loomed, and I needed someone to turn to. Fortunately, those times were few and far between, but there were times when one didn't want to burden those close to you, so who to turn to? It was those very difficult times when I found a true friend in God who, by then, I realised was always there and always ready to support and guide me towards better times; and He always did.

My journey had a number of roadblocks, the odd diversion, and took the occasional bypass, but now I feel that I'm on the motorway again and heading in the right direction. What final destination beckons? I shall just have to wait and see.

What I think I have learnt is that don't be afraid of setting out on a journey, even if you are not quite sure where you are going. There will be many signposts along the route, and it's just a case of spotting them before you take a wrong turn.

Perhaps It Just Takes Time?

"I'm not a Christian," the child exclaimed as he sought help
with his homework RE.
But how did he know, I thought to myself, when to me it
was clear that he was?
Why so adamant at that early age, and why so vocal as well?
Was it concern at what it might mean or what he might then
have to do?
With some sadness, I pondered these thoughts that I had and
wondered whether mine was the fault.
Should I have sown more positive seeds all those years ago?
… I just didn't know.
But to interfere would not have been wise, and I hope that
one day he will see
That there is something there, albeit not clear, in which he
can come to believe.

That he will find the love and support and friendship and
guidance,
The ever presence of God all around,
The One always there to turn to in strife,
The One there to lead him through life.

A Prayer for the Future

Dear Lord, I am saddened sometimes by the world we are
leaving for our children and grandchildren.

There seem to be constant reports of rising knife crime, the
rapidity of climate change, the risks posed by some social
media platforms,

and the continuing news of the willingness of some still to
go to war without having learnt the lessons of the past.

Where will it all end?

Life used to be so simple, but I guess that these days the
young would call that boring!

Help us all, O Lord, to introduce an element of sanity into
this crazy world in any way we can, even if that seems an
impossible task.

Every small act of kindness, understanding, or careful
guidance we can give can start to make a difference with
You beside us.

Deep down, I know that there is time to sow the seeds for a
better future if we start now.

Show me, Lord, what I can do today to start on this perilous
journey that, despite my sadness, I know is possible.

All this, Lord, I ask in the name of Your Son, Jesus Christ,
who, I am sure, saw the same issues in His day but rose to
the challenge and now hands the baton to each one of us.

Amen.

The Miracle Mystery

During Jesus' relatively short life, most agree He was about 33 when crucified, He performed many miracles. Scholars list a total of 37, starting with turning the water into wine and finishing with the second miraculous catch of fish at the Sea of Tiberius.

However, of these 37, there are six that end very differently from the rest. The majority of miracles are simply reported by one or more of the Gospel writers as happening, with their accounts of Jesus' life then moving on. But I want you to consider the following, which, to me, fall into two groups. The first is:

Jesus Casting Demons into a Herd of Pigs[1]

And then there are these five:

Jesus Cleansing a Man with Leprosy
Jesus Raising Jairus' Daughter Back to Life Jesus Healing Two Blind Men
Jesus Healing a Deaf and Dumb Man and
Jesus Healing a Blind Man at Bethsaida
Let's look at the last verse of each of these six reports. Firstly, Casting out the Demons. Mark concludes with:

"...go home to your friends, and tell them how much the Lord has done for you...."

---

1 Mark 5:1-20; Luke 8:26-39

In Luke:

"…Return to your home, and declare how much God has done for you…."

In all of the 32 readings, and in particular this one, there seems to be an acceptance that what Jesus has done should be acknowledged widely and His healing work publicised.

However, this varies considerably from the five other examples I have highlighted. Let's look at them in detail.

Jesus Cleansing a Man with Leprosy[2]

Matthew finishes by reporting:

"…Then Jesus said to him, '…See that you say nothing to anyone; but go, show yourself to the priest, and offer the gift that Moses commanded, as a testimony to them.'…." Mark concludes:

"…See that you say nothing to anyone; but go, show yourself to the priest, and offer for your cleansing what Moses commanded."

And Luke:

"…And He ordered him to tell no one. 'Go,' He said, 'and show yourself to the priest, and, as Moses commanded, make an offering for your cleansing.'"

---

2 Matthew 8:1-4; Mark 1:40-45; Luke 5:12-14

Jesus Raising Jairus' Daughter Back to Life[3]

Matthew closes with:

"...He strictly ordered them that no one should know this..."

and Luke with:

"...Her parents were astounded; but He ordered them to tell no one what had happened."

Jesus Healing Two Blind Men[4]

It is only Matthew who reports this miracle and ends his report with:

"...Then Jesus sternly ordered them, 'See that no one knows of this.'"

Jesus Healing a Deaf and Dumb Man[5]

It is only Mark who reports this miracle and ends his report with:

"...Then Jesus ordered them to tell no one..."

---

3 Mark 5:21-24, 35-43, Luke 8:40-42,49-56
4 Matthew 9:27-31
5 Mark 7:31-37

Jesus Healing a Blind Man at Bethsaida[6]

Here again, it is only Mark who reports this miracle and ends his report with:

"…Then He sent him away to his home, saying, 'Do not even go into the village.'"

Now my question is, why, having carried out the 37 miracles that were documented (and I guess there may have been others), did He choose the miracle of "Casting Demons into a Herd of Pigs" as the only one to specifically ask that they go out and tell everyone what had happened? More strangely, why specifically instruct those with Him at the other five miracles detailed above to say nothing to anyone about what had happened?

In all the things that Jesus did during His short life, I am sure that there is nothing He ever said or did that was not for a purpose. So why this? It has to be said that reading on from the reports of these particular events, it seems that those instructed not to say anything went out and told everyone anyway. Did Jesus know that that would happen, and it was a "cunning plan" to ensure the details were spread, as He knew folk would not keep those sorts of things secret? Perhaps that was so, but I've never really seen Jesus as a cunning operator; more a genuine, open, and honest sort of chap.

As I think I have said in some of my past musings, I don't have all the answers; I just ask the questions about things that have sparked an interest in me. Perhaps those who have spent a lifetime in matters ecclesiastical could proffer an answer? If so, please let me know, but only in words I can understand.

6 Mark 8:22-26

I'm afraid that great treatises including long words like eschatology, exegetical, homiletic are just beyond a bloke who failed his 11+!

God Bless

Epilogue

I do hope that my thoughts and feelings expressed in this little book will resonate with some. If it seems to have helped even one of you feel closer to God, it's been worth it. As time goes by, I will continue to put my thoughts on paper and maybe have a Volume 2 on the shelves one day.

God Bless,
Geoff